*Every poem has a story behind it but stories
cannot be poems*

Vivek.V

BLUEROSE PUBLISHERS
India | U.K.

Copyright © Vivek.V 2024

All rights reserved by author. No part of this publication may be reproduced, stored in a retrieval system or transmitted in any form or by any means, electronic, mechanical, photocopying, recording or otherwise, without the prior permission of the author. Although every precaution has been taken to verify the accuracy of the information contained herein, the publisher assumes no responsibility for any errors or omissions. No liability is assumed for damages that may result from the use of information contained within.

BlueRose Publishers takes no responsibility for any damages, losses, or liabilities that may arise from the use or misuse of the information, products, or services provided in this publication.

For permissions requests or inquiries regarding this publication, please contact:

BLUEROSE PUBLISHERS
www.BlueRoseONE.com
info@bluerosepublishers.com
+91 8882 898 898
+4407342408967

ISBN: 978-93-6261-775-0

Cover Design: Sadhna Kumari
Typesetting: Pooja Sharma

First Edition: June 2024

Every poem has a story behind
It but stories cannot be poems.......

"LIFE IS LIKE POETRY"

Αγάπη

INTRODUCTION...

Poetry are just experience for me I have been experiencing it for some year's. I think that it would be something different you have been read earlier; and I am trying here of making a summary of stories that would be not yet seen before. My theme of writing is that making you a curiosity in terms of poetry; these poems are a mix of stories and it will never ever finish and I make trying to introduce a different way and different style of writing.

Love it's like a Red Rose freshly sprung
in JUNE for- ROBERT BURS.

An emotion that never alters when it
Alternation finds for-WILLIAM SHAKSHEPRE.

Something that troubles your heart
For-THOMAS WYATT.

And for me it's PLATONIC!!!

Contents

FELT IN TEAR'S 1

ONE DROP OF LOVE 3

PAIN OF KILLS 7

LOVE 13

END 17

ARTIST 19

YOU 21

FRAMES OF LOVE 23

PARADISE 31

LIGHT 33

THE GIRL I FOUND 37

NIGHT 41

NATURE 45

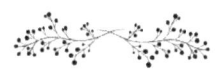

FELT IN TEAR'S

You were alone all night,

And the whole night was looking for you;

The night will pass.

In the dark of that night you tear's will also dip into it

The shining stars and the moon,

Become dull and gloomy they try to ask you,

The reason for the tears;

And the nights, the star's, the moon seems to be still dull and gloomy.

The crying face and the dark night's are similar,

Other than the night and tears nobody cares about;

Ridding through these nights are more beautiful than,

Seeing the day with someone who never bothers.......

TEARS WILL LET YOU INTO HAPPINESS....

ONE DROP OF LOVE

Just fallen through the crowd,

And the crowd seems to be busy;

The busy crowd with happy faces.

Everything seems to be regular,

But the street with crowd looks delightful

With children playing around

The street looks on a festival mode;

Candles and lamps are making ready for nights to shine.

But one who is still thinking all the day

No one minds, nobody cares, no one has noticed'

Because everyone is busy in festival mood,

Looks to be standing all that day.

The one who is waiting for the dearest one,
He looks to be tired and weak,
Standing the all day in sun
Morning passed, noon passed, evening passed-
And all around him is passing, other than him.

As he looks like to be a statue in the street
Nothing affects to him,
The dusty wind, the crowd rush, the heavy noise
Everything happened, but not even a single movement of him.

Is his love dead or gone to somewhere else?
Or she is dipped in the pains of love.
Other than God no one knows the truth,
The poor one still waiting for the dearest one.

LOVE CAN MAKE A PERSON EVEN MAD..

PAIN OF KILLS

You were in the waves of pain,

Pain will lead you to kill yourself-

And the reason for the pain;

Will be the one who you see's like your reaps.

Kills you in many ways,

But you must not even feel the pain inside

The pain kept inside is not even able to be cured

You had once in life it will be forever.

Many will hold the pain and go with it;

Some will break their thread-

In a pinch of time

It not be the curse for the wound

Some are killed for the existence

Others are killed for the lies to be kept,

No one is true to anyone

Everyone running for their life to be saved.

And every way of killing,

The hardest is by mind,

And if it comes from the favorites one's,

It will not able to hold.

The pain for the person, who hold it,

And the one killed by mind makes them into-

Break the thread, the one not killed by themselves-

That itself is a force from someone

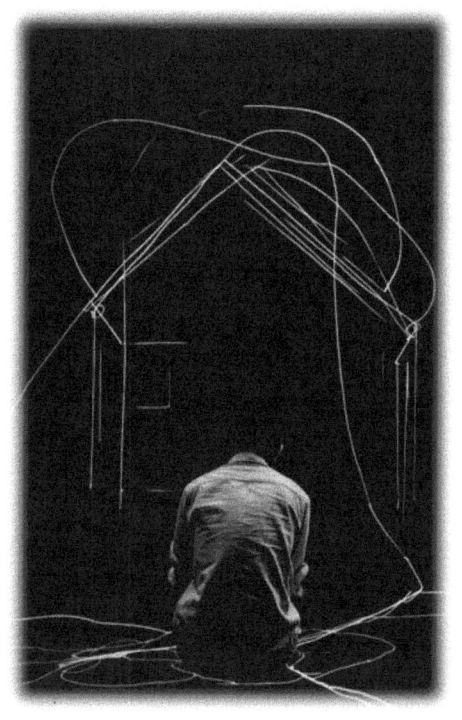

The person who have less will power
And who have soft hearted- mind
Cannot able to hold the pain
And in front of them no way.

They are like to be in the-
Middle of oceans
Winds and cyclones blow harder
No one can able to help them
Other than God no one could save them.

THE LAST ENEMY TO BE DESTROYED IS DEATH

-WORDS FROM THE BIBLE ...

PAINS ARE THE MOTIVATION TO MOVE FORWARD.......

LOVE

Words may never be enough,

To express this powerful. And yet;

Some of the most beautiful thoughts on-

Love has been expressed in our life itself.

Love may be pure or fatal,

Or it may be fleeting or eternal,

Other than it may be platonic or erotic,

At last it may not fit in to any categories at all.

Love is all in its varied forms-

Eternal, ephemeral , unrequited;

Platonic, erotic, ideal

And the most valuable one The Truth.

It's a feeling that considered seemingly indescribable,

Like a red rose freely sprung in spring,

An emotion that never alters when it alternates find;

And at last love is a valuable gift of god.

THE WORLD ITSLEF IS CONTROLLED BY -LOVE...

END

Everything has end-
End's for something new;
Reference to the title of premise you-
You call it madness, but i call it end.

The journey is not over yet-
Ends for some new beginnings;
Every ending will have a reason-
That reason gives you the end.

Some ending will have pain,
Those endings will teach some lessons
And that pain decides to move forward-
Or to be kept in quiet.......

ENDS ARE NOT BAD THINGS THEY JUST MEAN THAT SOMETHING ELSE IS TO BEGIN......

ARTIST

The free pencil can make her draw-
The beauty and fragrance of the nature.
The mind can make her draw-
Unfamiliar face gets unfamiliar mind.
The emotion can make her draw-
Unexpected drawings; get unexpected emotion.

That silent look-
That silent smile-
That silent laugh-
Makes the drawing more beautiful!!

The silent beauty-
Clear's all the entire fault in that......

THE BEAUTY OF THE NATURE IS DRAWINGS.....

YOU

It's just you- only you!!!

You make it everywhere every time,

Even the hot sun seems-

Like a shining stars in your presence.

Your smiling makes me-

Like the flowers that bloom's in a spring.

Seeing your laugh makes me-

Melt like the snow breaks in summer.

Seeing your tears makes me-

To see the drop of rain like the days of monsoon.

The days were bright when you was with me!!

And it were filled with happiness-

And everything seems to be like a story of imagination,

When would you make it again?

YOU ARE LIKE TO ME;

– THE EARTH WHO WAITS FOR MOON.

FRAMES OF LOVE

Love makes everything blind;
Blind makes changes,
And the changes affect in you-
And you will change too.

If it is true, just hold it;
Other than it's just drop it;
Let it be!
Nor it could be.

If it is true, you should hold it;
To hold it, you may,
Tell lies-upon lies
To your parents and others.

Your parents are the most loved ones of yours'
After they had become parents
They are living only for their children
And that's the world routine.

While loving someone you are-
Hiding it from your parents
Because of the age of yours,
And let not the smile of them disappears.

Maturity can be obtained at any time,
It does not matter what the age is-
Every second after you born-
Is a maturity period till the death.

Being in a young relation
Knowing from childhood
And loving each other
Doesn't makes wrong sense-

It's just a connection
After they succeed in their life
Then only they change into loving birds
Until then it's a bond to be kept.

But people around us make it wrongly,
Just frames stories badly
And the white dressed devils
Makes their beloved ones worry...

And if it get caught
Don't just follow the lies you told
Just let the truth be announced
That we are in love.

Love is a figment of our imagination
It's a matter of the heart,
Falling in love as a teenager is more in terms,
Than the experience in adulthood...

OUR WORLD ITSLEF IS A FRAMED STORY OF LOVE AND EMOTION..

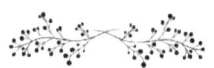

PARADISE

Paradise is a promise land

Their it's suffered accompanying sense of angel

It's be an elation place

And expected mist welkin.

Paradise is a place of harmony and love,

And society and worship

Place demon is among a divine court

And additional holy beings.

"THE PEACE EXISTS"

LIGHT

Light is universe-
The sun makes it;
The moon and stars do it,
Ultimately the universe.

Light is creature-
Living beings- grow and survive;
Without the growth nothing more,
Ultimately the creature.

Light is nature-
In darkness nothings blooms;
When the flowers blooms it spread colors,
Ultimately the nature.

Light is god-

Without light-nothing exists;

It's a source of energy

Ultimately the God.

THE UNTOLD TRUTH IN LIFE.

THE GIRL I FOUND

The girl i found thee,
Was she the angle from heaven?
With the glory of nature.

Her eyes were like shiny pearl,
Her beauty can make the world shine.

I could think that -
Was she the gift of god for nature?

I would like to fell in love;
But I could not able;
Her eye will make me still
And would never fall for her.

The time and hours passed,

And i would not yet talked to her,

But she was spreading the love and happiness,

Without my knowledge -

And i could never fell it out;

When the ray's felt on me-

It was just a dream.....

"THE WORLD MOVES FOR HER"

NIGHT

Night is something different,

But night with light is special;

And night with color is beauty

And night with sound makes the vibe.

A night can even make change-

Change the whole world.

Night catches everything.

The star, the moon, the earth

The night teaches us to dream;

If there is no night

Then how could we dream-

Together with the world.

Night makes the romance-

Night makes the love

Night makes the life

Night makes the nature...

NIGHT MAKES AND WE CELEBRATE IT OUT.

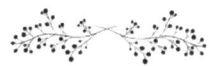

NATURE

The birds mingle with the trees;
And the tress with leaves,
Together their sound mix the heaven,
Why not I with thine!!

Nothing in the world is alone;
Everyone is together-
Everything is together-
Why not I with thine!!

See the bird's kisses high heaven,
The feather's clasp one another;
And the fishes clasps the sea,
Why not I with thine!!

NATURE LIVE'S;

-NOT US..

It runs through my vein, poetry in my heart
Lost in the world of words and verses
Life is a poem and I am the author.

www.ingramcontent.com/pod-product-compliance
Lightning Source LLC
LaVergne TN
LVHW061602070526
838199LV00077B/7143